This book belongs to:

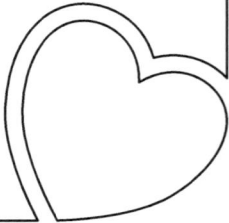

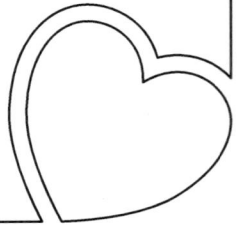

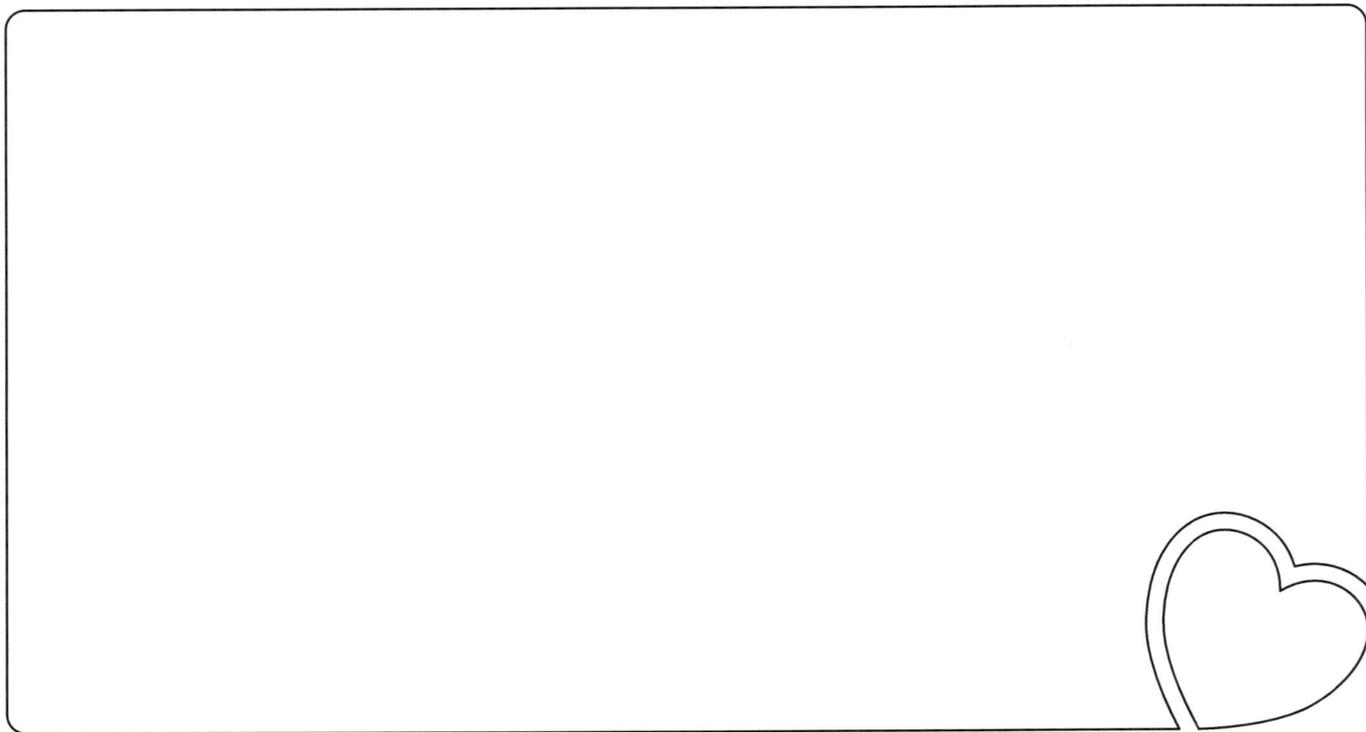

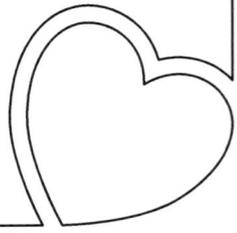

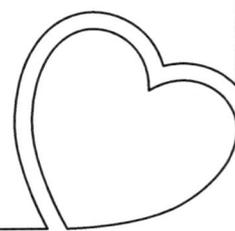

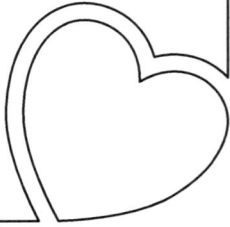

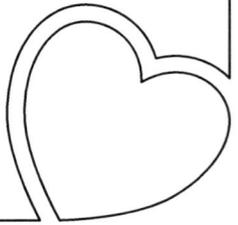

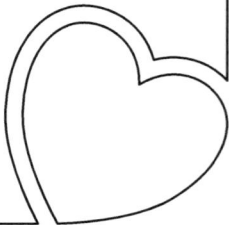

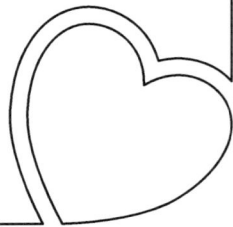

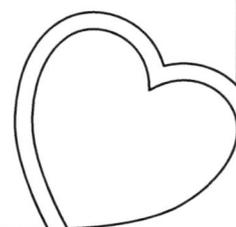

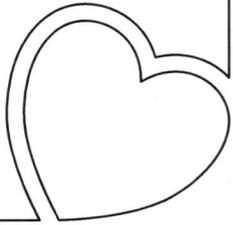

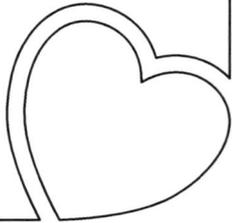

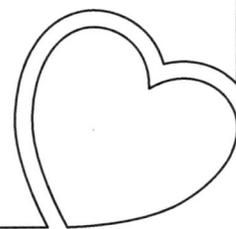

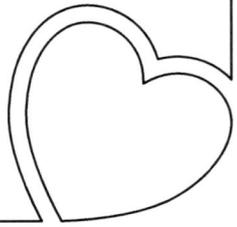

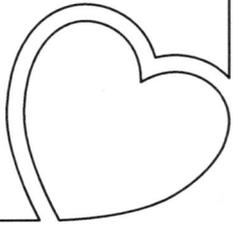

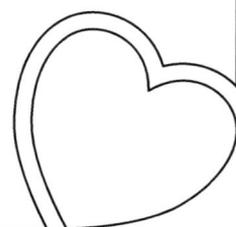

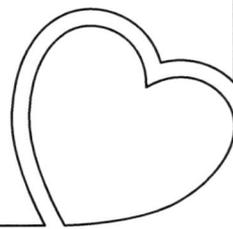

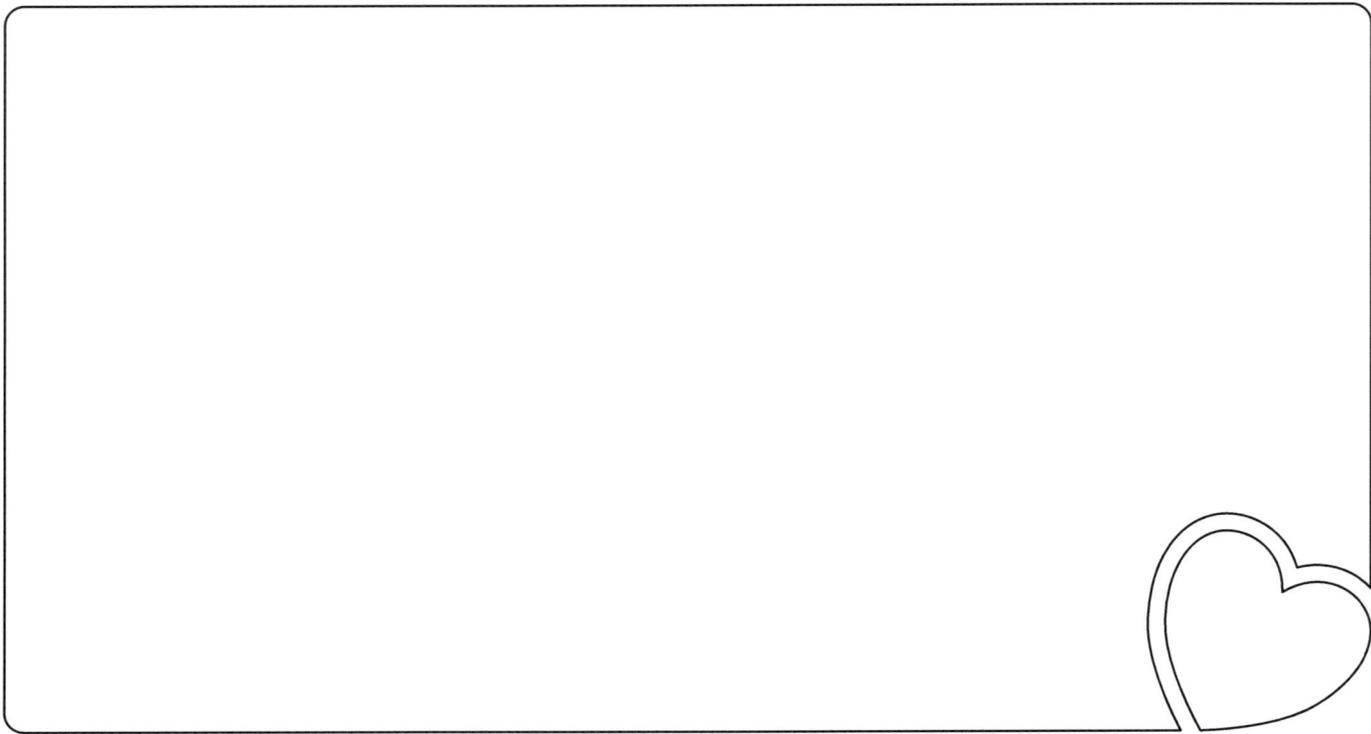

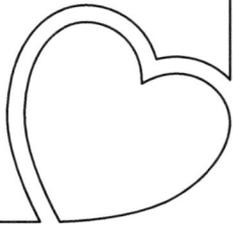

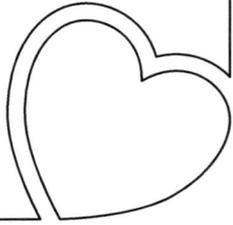

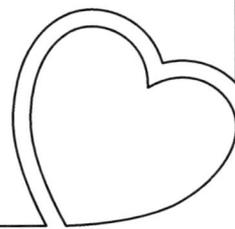

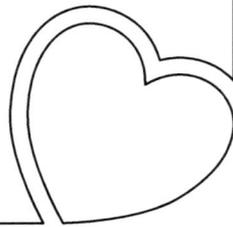

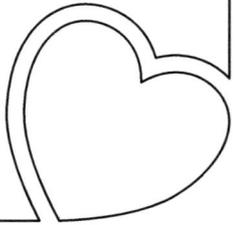

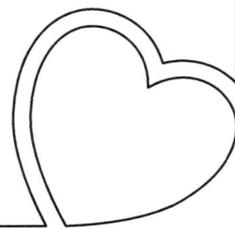

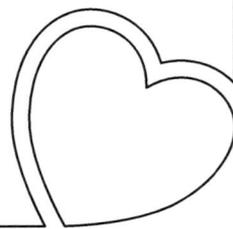

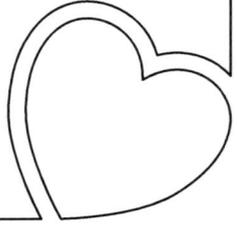

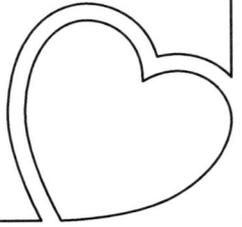

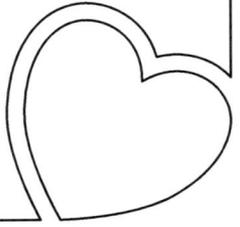

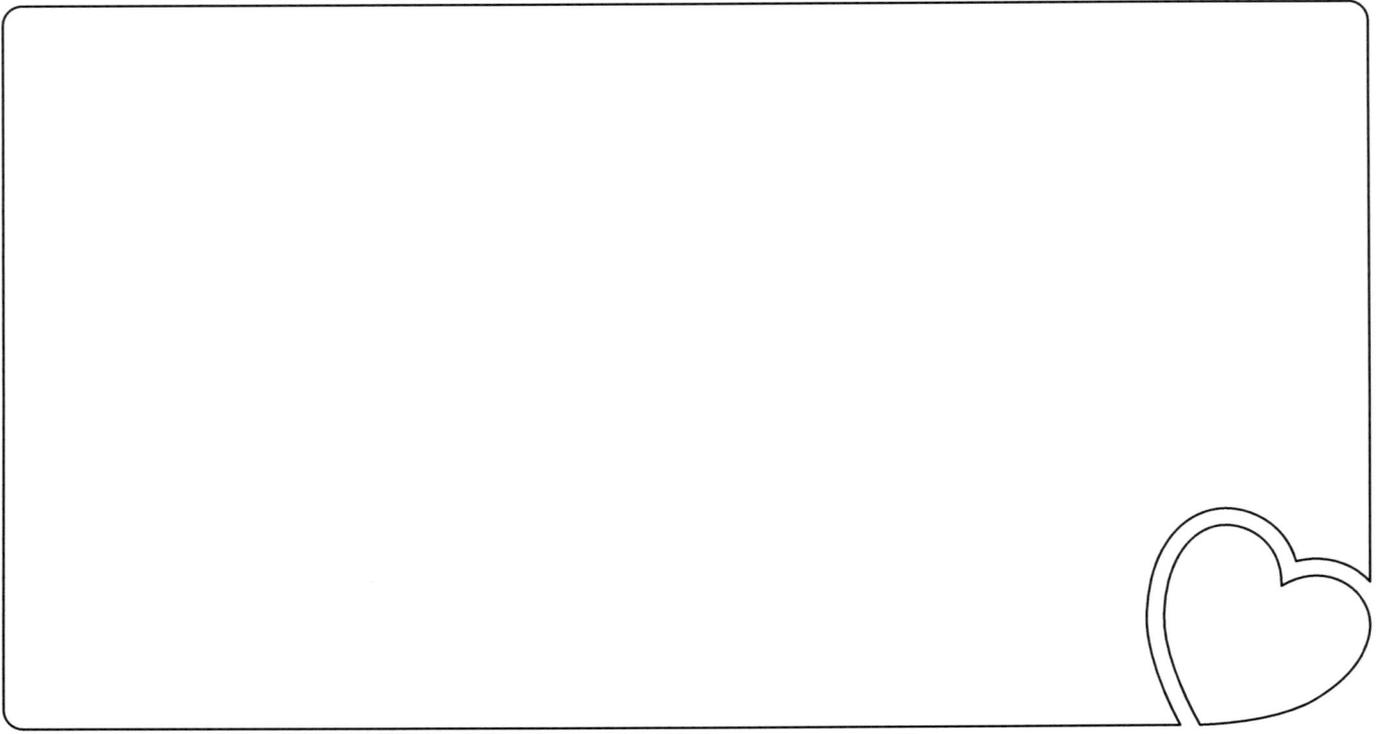

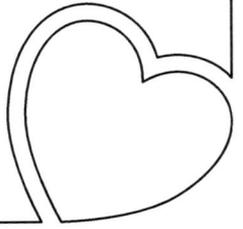

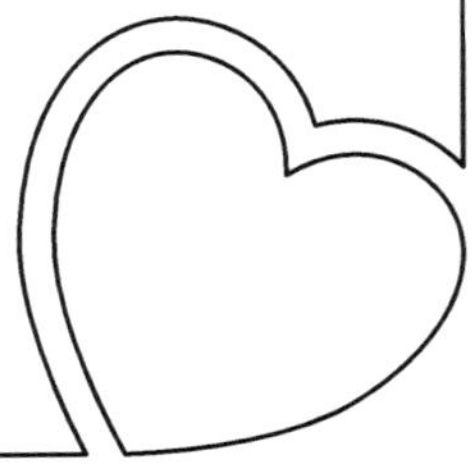

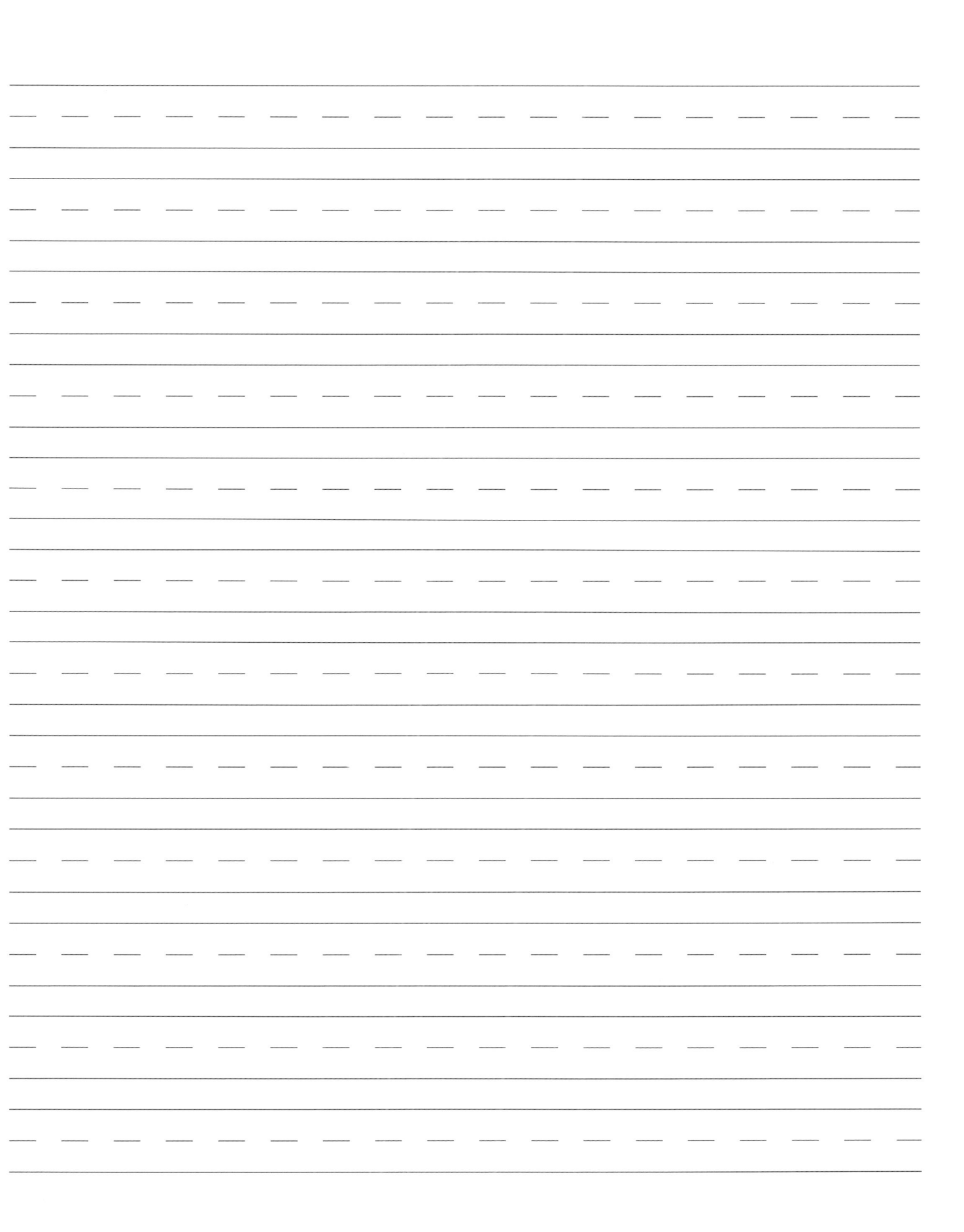

Made in United States
Troutdale, OR
09/10/2023

12794979R00066